METAMORPHOSIS

Writing from women at Serendipity

NY Writers Coalition Press
Winter 2015

Copyright © 2015 NY Writers Coalition, Inc.

ISBN: 978-0-9911174-8-2
Library of Congress Control Number: 2015931939

ALL RIGHTS RESERVED
Upon publication, copyright to individual
works returns to the authors.

Editor: Colleen Breslin
Layout: Anna Pettus, Rose Gorman
Title: The Serendipity Writers
Cover Image: Colleen Pierce Breslin
Interior Images: Colleen Pierce Breslin, Jeanne Byrne

Metamorphosis contains writing by members of NY Writers Coalition creative writing workshop for women at the Serendipity Program in Brooklyn's BedStuy neighborhood.

NY Writers Coalition Press, Inc.
80 Hanson Place, Suite 604
Brooklyn, NY 11217
(718) 398-2883
info@nywriterscoalition.org
www.nywriterscoalition.org

Serendipity is a residential program for individuals in the criminal justice system who have a substance abuse problem. It also welcomes walk-ins who are voluntarily seeking treatment. The Serendipity Program consists of individuals living together while they work through those personal and practical issues that block them from living fulfilling and drug-free lives.

Serendipity
944 Bedford Avenue
Brooklyn, NY 11205

Contents

INTRODUCTION: GATHERING
COLLEEN PIERCE BRESLIN   11

PART I: BURN

RANDOM SAND *JEANNE BYRNE*	16
MADONNA *KAELA AUGUSTINE*	17
WHAT IF *SHANNELY M. TRINIDAD*	18
TALL BROWN SKIN *JOYEIL GLOVER*	19
THANKS 2U *DOMINIQUE ALLEN*	20
CARMINE RED *KAELA AUGUSTINE*	22
ROAD TO OTAVALO *COLLEEN BRESLIN*	23
YOU ARE BEAUTIFUL *TARA D. RIVERA*	25
LOST CHILD *DOMINIQUE ALLEN*	26
NEW YEAR *SANDRA WILLIAMS*	27
LUCK *LOUISE BORRIELLO*	28
EXCITEMENT *GLORIA PAIGE*	29
LIBERTY *DOMINIQUE ALLEN*	30

PART II: SENSE

THE MOMENT *CELINES PARRA*	34
STYLEST *HOLLY M. WILLIAMS*	35
A DAY TO DREAM *DOMINIQUE ALLEN*	36
SUNRISE *SANDRA WILLIAMS*	37
CALM *SHANNELY M. TRINIDAD*	38
UNDER THE AUTUMN LIGHT	
DOMINIQUE ALLEN	39
COLD *LOUISE BORIELLO*	40
SUMMER *GLORIA PAIGE*	41
CRAZY *GLORIA PAIGE*	42
PATIENCE *GLORIA PAIGE*	43

WHAT IT FEELS LIKE TO STAND IN THE RAIN	
TARA D. RIVEERA	44
TIME OF MY LIFE GLORIA PAIGE	45
SUMMER DOMINIQUE ALLEN	46

PART III: REFLECT

THE FORGOTTEN JOYEIL GLOVER	50
WAILING CELINES PARRA	53
CRAZY KAELA AUGUSTINE	54
STRENGTH GLORIA PAIGE	55
FROM A DAUGHTER TO A MOTHER	
DOMINIQUE ALLEN	56
GOODBYE LETTER TO MOM	
TARA D. RIVERA	58
MISS ROSIE LOUISE BORRIELLO	69
GRANDFATHER SHANNELY M. TRINIDAD	61
NEW BEGINNINGS LOUISE BORRIELLO	62
MADONNA GLORIA PAIGE	63
FORGIVE ME GLORIA PAIGE	64
MY STORY JOYEIL GLOVER	65
A PERSON IN A PLACE WITH A PROBLEM	
GLORIA PAIGE	66
LIVING RIVALRY STEPHANIE KING	68
YOU ARE MY SISTER TARA D. RIVERA	71
MY BELOVED MOTHER TARA D. RIVERA	72

PART IV: WRITE

AT THE CAFÉ SANDRA WILLIAMS	76
ELECTION DAY GLORIA PAIGE	77
WHAT FILLS MY WRITING	
SHANNELY M. TRINIDAD	78
SWEET SPACE JEANNE BYRNE	79

A PERSON IN A PLACE WITH A PROBLEM HOLLY M. WILLIAMS	80
BELIEVE JOYEIL GLOVER	82
A NORMAL DAY GLORIA PAIGE	83
LINES CELINES PARRA	84
TRIBE SHANNELY M. TRINIDAD	85
DAWN JOYEIL	86
WHERE WOULD I FIND A SPACE TO WRITE TARA D. RIVERA	87
SOMETHING FOR RICHIE TARA D. RIVERA	88
CULTURAL TRUTH STEPHANIE KING	89
TRIBE JOYEIL GLOVER	90
A PERSON IN A PLACE WITH A PROBLEM TARA D. RIVERA	91

PART V: GROW

A BEAUTIFUL MOMENT KAELA AUGUSTINE	96
FAITH HOLLY M. WILLIAMS	97
MY CHANCE IS NOW SHANNELY M. TRINIDAD	98
MY WORK ELAINE G. SIMMONS	99
MY WORK LOUISE SORIELLO	100
THIS IS A STORY ABOUT PERSEVERANCE JOYEIL GLOVER	101
MY BEST FRIEND GLORIA GLORIA PAIGE	102
FREEDOM LOUISE BORRIELLO	103
ME TARA D. RIVERA	104
A WOMAN'S COURAGE CELINE PARRA	105
EXCITEMENT GLORIA PAIGE	106
DAWN TINA ARMSTONG	107
DETERMINATION DOMINIQUE ALLEN	108
MURAL THE SERENDIPITY WRITERS	109
ACKNOWLEGEMENTS	114
ABOUT NY WRITERS COALITION	117

Introduction

Gathering
Colleen P. Breslin

On the International Day of Happiness.

The air grew heavy but with a mass different from winter's weight. Grey wool sun captive slush sadness spinning globe. The women convene in a circle around the fire considering how ill-prepared they are, their city is, for spring. We are no longer we fear accustomed to airs of possibility and blades of grass reaching for new life to the the sky. Nine souls radiating, meditating in a community room named Luck in a house of recovery named Serendipity in the Bedford Stuyvesent section of Brooklyn. The Madonna - wise strong mother - was there also. Always emerging from the night shadows.

    Heat continues to rise. Goddamned global warming. Some fan their necks. Some remember icicles. Some lose themselves in the flame. We all breathe it. Suffocation takes hold of one of us.

Look out for one another.

    Blood slow its movement through her veins. We hear what she has told us. Blood pressure low, prescriptions showing their side effects, the heat feels too much. I am scared.

Continued

Women gather 'round.
　We feel her. With our pupils. Our hands. Our emotions. Our lungs. We grasp but with energy to respirate, we are able to cry out for our sister. In and out, we say. Help, we pray.
　It arrives. One grabs her coat. Another pleads for permission to ride this storm at her side. Another touches her, hand on upper arm, knee, down her damp t-shirt to the place behind her lungs, like her mother used to do. Others collect dollars so she does not leave broke. Still others visualize, calm the fire with their minds. All prayers on deck.
　Challenges exist first in our mind. Borne of memory, they rise up mountains, sound walls, flames in our paths. We may move through them or over them and eventually beyond them but doing demands determination. We may not deny them and we may not do it alone. No. We may not. Hold her up.
　Rise. Rise. Rise. Scenery unfolds to the mind's eye. Horizons impossible, now real. Clouds lose hold so high, the sun is warm. Bright. Who are you chatter says to fly so high? So close to the sun. How dare you?
　The atmosphere gets heavy. Memory weights us down, fear fires up. Our critical link she hardens and takes on heat, cycles furiously through oxygen. Force of nature. She. It occurs to her than as it had not moments earlier that the view before her is unfamiliar. Skin cells radiate aliveness, remind her of her nakedness. Spine stiffens. Shoulders pull back. Damn it, wings still incubating. Pain gusts, stings her eyes. They feel thirsty and begin to tire. They long to observe. For the creative period to end. She loses sight of her circle.
　She looks down to the place from which she came. To the place she once loved. The ground is a long way down. She obsesses about falling. We obsess about falling. She forgets freedom. We do also.
　We feel us feel her. Overcome. Overcome. Overcome. She hears us. Everything worthwhile is hard.
　Sojourner Truth. Borne in shackles. Baby girl whose mama spoke deep in to her eyes. Something different. Then disillu-

sionment. Pain. Journey. Found a place. Became new. Led us from slavery. Grew us a home.

    Cry. Wail. Mourn. Travel. Grow. Speak. Tell. Word. Freedom.

    Sojourn. To dwell for a time in a circle of love.

    Truth. That which is true.

    She dips. Dips. Dips. Down. All the women circle round. Hold her up. Scissor. Frog. Swimmer. Her feet begin to dance. She catches herself. She smiles. She smiles. She smiles. She smiles. She smiles. She smiles. She smiles. She smiles. She smiles. Nine times. The winds blow in. The rain comes down. The flame falls quiet. She flies. We fly.

Random Sand
Jeanne Byrne

She had gone for a short walk near the ocean shore line
and put her bare feet in the dry cool sand.
She felt herself as one with the universe.
Her body was in rhythm with each breaking wave.

When she stopped playing in the sand, she then felt how
 soft her feet were.
She came to the conclusion that the sand had made this so;
 and that it can be used to file nails and make other
 things smooth.
Looking more closely at the great sea of sand, she saw little
 grains of sand.
This made glass.

All of this is made from sand,
 which is really just old shells and stones which have
 been swept about in the sea.
When I see a bottle in the ocean, I think,
"Well, I guess it's going back to its birth place."

How many other things are made from sand?
What can you make from sand?
What can you find in the sand?

MADONNA
KAELA AUGUSTINE

Mystery,
Woven from the unique
Vibrant tapestry
of love, art, and war
she lives. Each layer unfolds
with the powerful tug
of paper and pen
ferocity unleashed.
Eyes learn sensitivity
when Madonna
meets their gaze,
seemingly captivated
by the sight of a phenomenal
    individual.
Ignorance attacks her self
of mahogany brown skin.
She remains unmoved
like sugar in the raw
She levitates above
with melodic grace,
the angelic spirit of she.

What If
Shannely M. Trinidad

If the world was in my hand,
What would I do.
What if I could take it and make it mine.
What if I took it and made it what I wanted.
What if I did as I pleased with it.
Would it be worth it, would it have changed me.
Today what if doesn't matter.
Today what if doesn't count.
Today what if is in the past,
Because what if doesn't count.
What if doesn't exist.

TALL BROWN SKIN
JOYEIL GLOVER

You can't tell from her walk that she is confident, when you see her walking in the street, you say to yourself, Damn, look at her,
TALL BROWN SKIN.

As she plays with kids on the playground, you would never understand how she moves, so smoothly that all you can say is, Damn, look at her, TALL BROWN SKIN.

As she moves closer to you, you start to think to yourself, Could this be the woman of my life who is TALL BROWN SKIN.

You reply to yourself, Yes, this is the woman of my life, this woman resides at Serendipity. And she is a Tall Beautiful Woman that has her own goals and loves herself today.

Want to know who that TALL BROWN SKIN woman is?

You need to ask her.

THANKS 2U
DOMINIQUE ALLEN

Used and abused by many,
Loved and adored by few.
All these things I felt
Because of you.
If only you knew all of the pain
I have been through.
Mom, why couldn't you
Love me as much as I loved you.
I beat myself up
Trying to be who you wanted me to be.
But slowly killing my soul and myself
Being someone who I didn't want to be.
Now it's time for me to believe,
To spread my wings
And soar like an eagle in flight.
Sometimes like a phoenix in the sun
Shining so bright.
Throughout all my life,
I had to fight.
To this day,
I still fight.
I fight for my life.
My freedom.
My kids.
My family.
My sobriety.

Loved and adored by many,
Always hated on by a few.
All these things are because of you.
Mother, if only you knew
All of the turmoil I have been through.
You should have realized
The hurt you caused, and how
I use it to make it to another day.
All the negatives turned to pluses for me.
I think of the abusive days
So I can push myself away and out of the rut.
To a mother who doesn't care,
Good luck.
Now when I'm stuck, I will pick myself back up.
As of this minute,
Loved,
Adored,
Cared for,
Listened to by Many.
(I don't think about the negative few).

CARMINE RED
KAELA AUGUSTINE

The sunset exposes a passionate illustration that only she could relate to. Every evening she finds herself welcome in the window sill, enthralled by its captivating beauty. She can't help but gravitate towards the fire orange and scarlet hues. Each ember bursts with color that tells a wordless story, painted with the brush of pleasantries. Not only does she find comfort in the sight but she feels a brighter beginning approaching the horizon. After all, the sun only sets before it rises.

Road to Otavalo
Colleen P. Breslin

Development is a human right.
A bridge brought up green and strong.
The best erection the region's ever seen.
Besides the aqueducts.
No temples here.
Chemados lest they be occupied.
He leans against the bridge's green leg,
Stripes on his shirt fade into flower.
Escolares buzz by.
Clouds like cotton balls gather overhead.
Stretch. Unravel. Roll.
Light bright formations.
Shadows then and the drizzle.
Lavando from his hard hat
Film that smells like smog.

Ravines ravined in search of gold.
Hillside his home spring their source.
Infrastructure spins domestic manufacture
Excavators hook up to arms imported
Pipes explore deep inside.
The touch a torment.
(This will only hurt a bit),
She spits sand and gravel until finally.
Like blood, it flows.
Her irritated pores close up.
What once was green is now the cost.

Continued

Jackhammers intubate.
Steel piles respirate.
Guitars sing.
Whiskey flows.
Flamboyants paint.
Century cacti bloom.
The circus comes to town.
A story ages gold
Blooms with the century cacti.
Here.
Now, all the region is a desert.
All the desert is a stage.
What comes next.

Stages of addictions mimic the stages of grief.
A bus coughs up.
His ride.

You Are Beautiful
Tara D. Rivera

I am beautiful inside and out. I love everything about me, from my eloquence to the very way I put on a scarf. From my youthful spirit, to the woman I have shown myself to be. I love everything about me, my curvy body to my sexy eyes that tell so many stories, eyes that show all the way to my soul. I am beautiful inside and out. I love everything about me. I see past my flaws because I know deep down that I have the ability to discover and accept them on my own, and that is what makes me so flawless to me. I am beautiful and I love <u>everything</u> about me.

Lost Child
Dominique Allen

Born and raised in a hood called Brownsville where they keep it trill. Hold up homie, Don't let it spill. Pissy elevators, broken bottles as I walk down the street. Aimlessly, like a lost child.

Always fighting, letting them things ring off, just after poppin' bottles and wanna be models with not much education. Just like me, they are someone's lost child.

I want from puffin' black-n-mild and smokin' some loud. Where the fuck did that shit come from. I guess another lost child who ran wild.

No longer lost, this child has found her own way to live life. Still keepin' it trill but with more intelligence and support from the cheerleader within.

Real recognize real because don't have time for the fake.

NEW YEAR
SANDRA WILLIAMS

Right now, I'm having a hard time adjusting to
change; but I feel I'm in a safe place where
I can be able to be at ease to learn more about
different ideas, different new beginnings.

Having had skills to work
At one time, those
Enable me to contribute to my living situation.

And then, Life threw me a hard ball
And now I'm trying to soften it,
And grab what's here
At my fingertips.
So I can move on.

Luck
Louise Borriello

That was good luck.
The day I found my ring
That was good luck.
When I won the lottery
That was good luck.
Getting that job
That was good luck.
Not getting robbed
That was good luck.
Surviving the storm
That was good luck.
Catching that last bus.
I'm a very lucky person.

EXCITEMENT
GLORIA PAIGE

How exciting it is to be free from addiction. To see and smell the beautiful flowers, where in addiction, there was no scent at all.

How exciting it is to see birds, with the rainbow colors on their necks, where in addiction they looked dirty and dingy.

How exciting it is to wake to the bright yellow sun in the crystal blue sky, peaking through the cotton-like clouds, where in addiction every day and everything is filled with darkness and drear.

Ahh, how exciting it is to wake up and have a chance to live again.

LIBERTY
Dominique Allen

On my way to the place they call America, the land of the free and the home of the brave. The first thing I see is a lady called Liberty, Stand as tall as can be on her wonderfully set stage.

She whispers to me to come sit and tell me about your journey. I roll out my blanket and tell her how bad I want to be free. She told me whenever you feel stuck, look for me with my torch burning bright and you will gain some insight on why we can be free and why they call me Lady Liberty.

The Moment
Celines Parra

A beautiful moment is the most wonderful feeling we can only cherish in a moment when you can come into peace with yourself and that wonderful feeling that brings you back alive again to that moment.

STYLEST
HOLLY M. WILLIAMS

One brain, two braids, three brains, four.
How lovely the style.
Braid it up, comb it down
How sweet the smile.
I twisted and pinned it up,
Even let it grow wild.
I curled it and shaped it,
To a classy idle.
It's never too much to add or even,
Let it hang for awhile.
I can't stop or even think but to experiment a style.
Even for a child.
For chemistry has taken me on a long ride
So I cut and I trimmed and shaped it into a pile.
This is a job, that's never down.
So I will take up where I left off tomorrow.

A Day to Dream
Dominique Allen

As the rain started to fall, the aroma of the earth begins to awaken my senses. As my body becomes restless, I start to pace my bedroom floor, daydreaming about the fun I can have even on this rainy day.

I daydream about Rapunzel waiting for someone to save her sitting, sitting, waiting through the sun and rain, I can imagine the pain. I feel a need to explain but I will leave it for another day.

SUNRISE
SANDRA WILLIAMS

The sun came up and it was calm.
I could see a colorful shade of rays
Shining in the sky
Put me in the frame of mind as that
Peaceful could I have seen,
Could I have imagined.

Calm

Shannely M. Trinidad

The sun came up and there was calm. We as newborns know nothing of the world.

We are taught everything we ought to learn. We grow up being our parents' Love and Pride.

We try to be humble and joyful, have serenity within toward what we were raised to be. And how to act. Every morning as the sun rose, I'd look out the window. Inhale. Take in the peace and calmness around me. My mother taught me that. Everyday as the sun came up and I felt that calm. I knew that from what I learned growing up. Everyday is a new day. To not care for tomorrow, that the sun will shine again and I will feel that calm.

UNDER THE AUTUMN LIGHT
DOMINIQUE ALLEN

My face begins to brighten as I am awakened by the autumn light. I wash my clothes and hang them on a line to dry and here comes a sparrow soaked, wanting to get dry by the autumn light. I grab a nice cold beverage a lawn chair and to the porch I go, to curl up with a good book under the autumn light. As noise turns to silence and crickets start up band practice, I start to stargaze into the autumn night.

COLD
Louise Boriello

Bundled up
Winter
Red nose
Getting sick
Boots
Ice
Beer
Ice Cream
Cold Water
Shiver
Frost bite
The Arctic
Long Johns
Ice Skating
Skiing

SUMMER
Gloria Paige

Picnics
Bar-b-cues
Go to the Beach
Going to water parks
Going to amusement parks
Shorts and tank tops
Parades and carnivals
Sightseeing
Laying on the grass
Hanging with friends
Movies
Enjoying hot, sunny days
Playing in the street with fire hydrant water on.
Ices, Smoothies, Ice Cream Trucks

CRAZY
GLORIA PAIGE

What's Crazy?

   P
      E
         O
            P
               L
                  E

PATIENCE
Gloria Paige

Having patience can be hard to do.
Not having patience can bring an array of
    unwanted emotions
(anger, bitterness, to start)
You can't sit still.
Can't think straight.
Anticipating for things to happen quickly.
Fast.
If we could learn to slow down just a little a bit,
We would see the benefits of just practicing patience.
While we are rushing,
We miss out on the blessings.
Patience is truly a virtue.

What It Feels Like to Stand in the Rain
Tara D. Rivera

As I take a walk out into the street, I close my eyes. I imagine myself to be in the middle of nowhere, where there are plenty of trees and enormous skies. I can feel the wind blowing through my hair, straight down my back to my feet that are bare.

As a single drop sets off the storm, I can feel my insides take on a rare form. All of my emotions of sorrow and pain seem to have trickled down the drain.

Just one feeling is left, that feeling called LOVE. As it pours down upon me from the heavens above. As I jump and dance and sing in the rain. Not a care nor a worry intrudes my brain. My soul is at peace, not one trouble there remain. That is what it feels like to stand in the rain.

Time of My Life
Gloria Paige

I knew I was in for the time of my life.
It was when spring comes,
there is so much to enjoy.
Picnics, barbeques, going to theme parks,
and looking at the beautiful array of f lowers.
Watching yellow sunny days,
picking through white clouds behind the baby blue skies.
Children playing in the park,
people jogging at Central Park;
just lying on a blanket on the smell of green grass,
having lunch with the sound of soft tunes on your radio.

She knows she is in for the time of her life when Spring comes.
The weather is nice. Insects are crawling about,
walking into the webs of spiders so lovely spun.
Lovely days ahead, all season long, rain or shine.

SUMMER
DOMINIQUE ALLEN

Oh what a wonderful delight! The hot and steaming sun rays. Bouncing off trees and plants, bringing life to the earth. Let's not forget the tans and people walking around with their sun-kissed skin. What about the beaches. Look at how the families flock to them with smiles and giggles, in their tummy is little tickles. Hey, look over there, that cotton candy. Wait, hold on, look over there, a school of dolphins jumping so high into the summer heat but for me in the pool or in the cool AC is where I will be.

Reflect

THE FORGOTTEN
JOYEIL GLOVER

Dear Judge:

    I am writing on my thoughts of the abuse of which they treat the mentally ill when it comes to the criminal justice system. I would like to start by saying I am a thirty-three year old mother of two. I have been diagnosed with Bipolar Disorder with Manic Depression and Mood Disorder. At the age of thirty-three, I was also diagnosed with Schizophrenic Psychosis. I was not properly diagnosed until the age of thirty-three.

    I can remember when I had my first daughter. I went through a lot of changes in my pregnancy, a lot of it was due to my mental health. I can recall a time when I went to the psych ward for postpartum depression. I didn't know that I could be affected just by giving birth. At the time, I was living in a mother and child shelter. It may have been a time I was giving my baby girl a bath at night, and I had dropped her by mistake. As a result of my mishandling her, they tried to make an ACS case out of it, all because she had a little hole in her head that eventually closed up. Then three years later, I gave birth to another baby girl and I started showing the same systems, but I was able to get the help early in my pregnancy. When I went into the DV shelther, I had lost both of my girls due to my mental illness. What made me take a look at the judicial system different was when the judge in my case said, "I don't understand why your mothers who have a mental problem think you can keep having babies. My thoughts are you all should be spayed or fixed."

When this was said to me, I felt like someone was judging me for giving birth to two beautiful little girls. It wouldn't hurt if she would have asked to speak to me and she might have noticed that I am a smart mother, a good person and a wonderful daughter. For awhile after that, I contemplated suicide for how the judge made me feel.

The reason why I say the judge is wrong is yes, I acknowledge that I had a problem with drugs and alcohol. Yes, I am getting the help I need. Not just for my drug addiction but for my mental health issues. It has been a long time coming for me but what, I am here and I am alive. Oh yes, I take care of my daughters by taking my medication and accepting help for my health.

I am in recovery due to a drug problem. That is also due to going off my medication. We are not bad parents or people. My reason for writing this is to let you know that the laws and the way that you treat us need to change. Now I am on my meds and getting clean off of drugs and I am becoming a better mother, daughter, wife and person. I live in a MICA program which is helping me deal with all of my issues. You know I have been searching for a place that could help me and I found one. If you all could build more places like this instead of putting us in jail or psychiatrics wards, we could become productive citizens. All you need to do is take the time and talk to us. There are JUDGES, LAWYERS, DOCTORS who suffer from mental illness and they are able to work, raise a family. Please I am asking you to just stop prejudging us and spent the time to get to know us. Like I said in the beginning, my name is Joyeil Leatrice Glover and I am mother of two girls and their names are Miracle Leatrice Glover and Alexis Channel Glover and I am

Continued

a great mother. At the present time I am at a place called Serendipity II and yes, not only does it help with the mental, it also helps with my drug and alcohol addiction that I am overcoming.

So with all of that being said, I say unto you, please the next time, think about judging or throwing the book at a person, take the time and ask whether he or she has an illness that they need help on. These are my pleas to you all. Take the time and get to know us and walk a step in our shoes before you shut the door on us.

Thank you.

Wailing
Celines Parra

Wailing on
Takes me to destiny
Brings me back to the future of our lords.
And reminds me off hell
So that I can guide my soul.

Crazy
Kaela Augustine

She stares at the mirror, unfamiliar with the woman looking back at her. Looking through her, past her swollen lip and shattered cheek bone. She's lost herself, just as she lost her ability to smile. Soul searching with dirty hands, fingers drenched in the template of her own crimson red blood, the key to her salvation is round in the confined chamber of the medicine cabinet. Her mental abode entitled freedom, in the shape of a book, made of flames. She turns to face her demise, a room coated in gasoline and men's clothing, with sparks in her irises. Grasping on to the matchbook for dear life, a life she never knew or appreciated. She strikes back, striking a more powerful blow than anything she'd ever endured became her passion. Her crazed obsession was fulfilled when she took control of her life. Simply by taking another. Strike. You're out!

STRENGTH
GLORIA PAIGE

Only the strong survive. Yes, it's true. When you have been through situations you thought you would never get out of. Being touched inappropriately as a child and being afraid to tell someone because no one will believe you. Feeling weak, defeated will now rise when in sight. The one you thought would love you, and never hurt you is beating you up, giving you black eyes, broken ribs, and you don't have the strength to leave because he says he will kill you. But if you don't stand up and fight, find courage and strength and say no more, you will not survive. Like I said in the beginning, only the strong survive.

From a Daughter to a Mother
Dominique Allen

I'm writing you to let you know how I feel. Well, I feel so good. Despite the fact that I'm just like you. I abandoned my kids, like you did to me. I don't care about anyone but myself and all of the man-made things I came to cherish. And because of this I don't know how to love. Every time a man says he loves me, I say I love him too and I go out and cheat or never return. If you want to know why, I will tell you. It's because you said you loved me and turned your back on me. You left me all alone for your own selfish needs and wants. Did you know I was being abused since I was a toddler? Of course you know. I told you before but you turned a blind eye and my cries fell on deaf ears. I looked up to you when I found you but look where I am now, starring to be loved by a mother. Crying because I miss my kids and drinking and drugging not to feel these things. If only you knew the pain I'm going through, maybe you would look for me. Or maybe not because of your greed. Since my daddy died, I wanted to be greedy, greedy for hugs and kisses and most importantly, love. Not just any love, the love only a mother could give to her child in need. That's a mom indeed. All I have to remember you are painful memories. I hear your voice, it still fills my head and this is what it says, "you nasty dumb bitch, you are not my child." Without a mother, this child has gone wild. Instead of being a productive member of society, I am another number of the statistics chart. Another mother who forgot who she is, and who she can be. But guess what, I have someone who wants me for me but I won't let it be. He wants me to be me and to forget you and all of the pain you have caused. I constantly remember that without hate, there won't be love. You can forgive but you won't forget. So today, after all is said and done, you will stand for God to judge. Unto this day, I pray for you with all my might, and I love you with all my heart. I have always loved you from the start. Now my days are shorter and the life I always wanted is soon to come. I got a new love, my kids, a man, soon to be married and raise our family. Learning what love is was a journey for me. Especially in and out, in and out of abusive relationships, running for my life. *Oh, how I won't forget that cold winter night.* I wish you could just see my two beautiful girls, the youngest is seventeen months old and looks just like you. To this day I love them and you, no matter what. So when my big day is set, I will be sure to invite you and show you how strong and beautiful I am and my love for you. This letter may have caused some feelings but the one question that still burns in my heart, why did you leave me? If you decide to answer or not, I still forgive you and love you. That's how strong a mother's love is. I miss you.

Goodbye Letter to Mom
Tara D. Rivera

Dear Mom,

By the time you get this letter, you will be someplace better. A place that is far away, where you can stay for infinity. You know it was your destiny. Somewhere that is white and fluffy a place, where there are no tomorrows, only better todays. A place where you gaze through the eyes of angels. I know you see us. We're making you proud without being loud. We got it right. We tried our best not to fight. I can see you smiling before I close my eyes at night. I can see your imprint in the sky "So you got your wings." I knew that you would. You've always been good, as good as you could.

As I look back at your time here on earth, you have always been special. Since the very moment of your birth, you have always loved people and they adored you too. You surely had a way with making people laugh when they were sad and blue. So I say to you Mom, fly away with those angels and live eternal life, where there is not strife, no faction, no friction, no conviction but freedom, freedom to be you.

    The father has something for you. It's your new heart. The one you were anxiously waiting for. Well, you'll have to wait no more. Now you are complete. You have everything you need. Now I understand why you were so happy the last day I saw you. I couldn't put my finger on it but you knew, I saw the flow. I now understand it was your time to go. We'll stick together Mom, just as you request. It may not always be perfect but we'll do our best. Time for me to end now. You know the rest. I will always love

MISS ROSIE
LOUISE BORRIELLO

Do you remember when
You were beautiful and happy?
Now your hair is nappy.
Do you remember when
You started the day with a smile.
Now that is torn in pieces,
Thrown in a pit.

Do you remember
How we laughed and sang.
These memories are happy for me.
But bring you pain.
Miss Rosie, please come back to life.
Oh, what a gain.

GRANDFATHER
SHANNELY M. TRINIDAD

To think I sought out the day to see you again.
To think that you'd see me again, be proud of me.
To believe there was more.
For the end to come and the days get longer.
You're no longer here,
You no longer can feel the pain.
You are in a better place in my heart, deep inside
Where I can remember you,
Just the way you were.
'Till we meet again,
Your love will be my savior,
And you, my angel from above

New Beginnings
Louise Borriello

New beginnings come at different times in our lives,
Like the first time I learned to drive.
New beginnings make you nervous,
But each one has a purpose.
I moved out of my house.
I got my first real job.
I moved to Staten Island.
I became a "stepmom."
(Oh, how I hate that word).
My greatest new beginning
Was the day I got married.
Oh boy, on that day,
I was very harried.

MADONNA
Gloria Paige

She has been through it all. As a child, teenager, an adult, she has been through so many adversities, you would never think she would have the courage to write her story. This is short story about how she survived. Molestation, incest, rape and domestic violence, just to name a few. Domestic violence was one of the toughest challenges she had to face. You see, she is a survivor. At the hands of her abuser for many years, she thought her only way out was suicide. God had other plans for her and made her escape her torture by freeing her, letting her escape by walking out and never turning back around. The domestic violence, along with the addiction she suffered for 19 years, is finally over. She finally got relief and help through RX, therapists and ongoing care. Madonna is strong and most definitely a survivor.

FORGIVE ME
GLORIA PAIGE

God, please forgive me for my sins I committed today. For allowing Satan to take me out of my character. I should have known better being a woman and child of God. This is what I pray every morning, to let others be who they are but love them anyway. God, please give me the strength to get me through this process of recovery. Continue blessing me with a humble heart, loving heart and rid my heart of anger. Fill my heart and soul with your holy spirit. Keep my covered with your wings and thank you for dying for my sins so I can be forgiven.

MY STORY
JOYEIL GLOVER

There once was a little girl who I knew. She was molested from the time she was little and until her early teenage years. She had an abortion at the age of ten. The girl kept finding herself in and out of bad, abusive relationship. This girl dealt with a pimp, an abusive husband, also turmoil with her mother, and the boyfriends her mother kept picking. She became an addict, just so she could stop feeling or even thinking about the pain. She had an awakening one day and on that day is when she finally said, "enough is enough."

A Person in a Place with a Problem
Gloria Paige

As she lay on the cardboard box on the icy sidewalk, you can tell she is cold and hungry. Her long gray hair is disheveled and in locks. You can see that it hasn't been combed. As you look at her face, you see a tired, old woman with rotten and missing teeth. Her clothes are too big, layered, torn and the smell of toxic. She has on one shoe too small with her enlarged toes, protruding through the sides. Her other foot is swollen, dirty with open sores and wounds. Infection oozing out with the odor of death in the air. She has a cup in her hand and sign in the other that reads, "Please help me, I'm hungry and homeless." She is on the streets of New York City.

Most people pass her by and look at her with pity, while others with a caring heart drop money in her cup and give her leftover, half-eaten food from their lunch. She is grateful and thankful. She starts to feel a little hope. Minutes later a big, white van with large orange letters on the side with the "BRC" pulls up alongside of her. It is an organization who helps take homeless people off the street. No matter what problems you may have, whether it is psychiatric or medical, people who have mental illnesses, alcoholics, addicts or some who are just down on their luck. They give her a safe place to stay. Food and shelter. They let her bathe, wash, cut her hair and give her clean clothes. They also give her medical and psychiatric attention. They address all of her needs.

Now, two years later, she has her own place, a job with BRC, helping people who were just like her. A person in a place with a problem.

LIVING RIVALRY
STEPHANIE KING

I take up too much space? Really? No one had ever thought it appropriate to share that before. I thought I was just one person, but apparently my son or rather, having had a son was just absolutely too much, mental hostility interpreted by heuristics of the other members of the house to grapple with or entertain as difference--possibly even marginal--for even a brief second. As a birth mom, the second time I saw my son after leaving the hospital was that summer. I left Brooklyn only for a week while living with rivals who were perched in an illegal apartment.

Now, I can't write. Overcome them first. Disregard the tears by the thousands over situations strikingly similar with mistakes made by know-it-all brats who attend college and drop out of Ivy League PhD programs, have trust funds they burn with alcoholism, hell, have parents who acknowledge their existence without trying to be owed something from the child. In my writing space I hear others like me--the exploited, bullied, and dead serious--who devise the logic behind group forces without the total farce, but it isn't a shortcut. The social psychology is rampantly ignored in favor of shortcuts and interpolations are are unethically placed.

I can understand colonized bodies. I am one. I do not protrude falsehoods and fashion identity politics as a meme. This rivalry between roommates was a fight for ignorance and a fight for radical space. I wanted them to see the latter option. The overt message was already clear to me. "We're bourgeois." She told me she had read Foucault. She wanted the same thing the other members wanted--my money--but more of it and she knew what I was doing to make it. I was asked to relinquish her deposit with sex work money after I discovered that the whole apartment was a fire trap, illegal, and we didn't have to pay rent there. Ha. Never mind a simple "thank you".

To make matters worse, the manic of the house had strewn crap all over the living room upon my return, and I was accused of coming off curtly to her for telling her I wouldn't pay rent until she cleaned it up. She, on the other hand, was angry all the time and could barely have a conversation without a delusional accusation. Forget asking her to take care of shared space when she was the one who had made a mess. She routinely would 'deep' clean in a housewife mode, but thought that it bought her something of her own right to demolish in between her fixes. I knew they were all psychotic. Before I ever wrote a word of this story, she accused me of writing it in a "way", and I still have no idea how she compares that she isn't a Nazi.

When I returned from my visit with my son I had to address the issue of not transferring rent into a private bank account held by the ring leader. I had agreed to an escrow account. I don't understand what was so hard about that to comprehend. Trust issues and poor humor. They were just plain wrong, but it was a joke to their privilege. I wish I didn't have to remember these people. The level of disgust I feel still boils over when I recall how excited and giddy they became by the simple conflict they created.

A cult leader would have tried to hide their true intentions better than this. So, I told them that, but only after I sat two of them down to speak about the personal account and the obvious risk of them stealing my rent for their own use. I mean, there is absolutely no protection against giving someone money directly without a written agreement--and that's exactly what they wanted from me--absolute pillage. They told me I couldn't be part of the "community" when I disapproved of the option I was given. To say the least, I respond-

Continued

ed curtly. Again, they laughed at me. When was the right time to hold back the trust?

The obsessive thoughts occupied my brain for weeks that turned into months until the day before my birthday, and then holding onto the last second, eviction. They were long gone, having made a deal out of complete and utter denial and weakness. I found a pro bono lawyer who believed in my potential housing case law due to the Marshall's exercise of his own discretion. We fought as hard as we could to make the judge realize it, but in the end it failed, and all I could do was let in the Department of Buildings and the Fire Department at the very last minute so that the owner of the building would be hit with the fines, and they were enormous. As far as I know, a roommate--not on the lease--case law against Marshall discretion is still necessary and unfulfilled, but entirely possible.

During the legal battle over the housing rights attached to the apartment, I had no space to write, but I had the whole place to myself once the lease holders and their roommates were gone. Still reeling over the eviction paperwork discrepancies that they tried to oust me with and on a specific day that they wanted despite my rights, I was alone, but glad I wasn't in the company of unauthentic martyrs, who more or less, were fascists. Never again.

You are My Sister
Tara D. Rivera

You are my sister. We share the same mother. You are my sister. I would never trade you for another. You are my sister. We share the same heart. There once was a time in our lives we were never apart. You are my sister. We shared the same pain. You are my sister. We share the same family name and then the time came when we took different lanes. I was going too fast, things were never the same. You walked high. I walked low. The unity we once shared, where did it go?

I never meant to hurt you. Perhaps I was moving too fast. Come back to me, sister. Our love was a bond to last. A lifetime of laughter. A lifetime of pain. Come back to me sister. I've so much to gain.

I miss you so much. I miss your sisterly touch. You need to know, sister, that I am still here, waiting for you on the land where we took our own paths through life. Just remember, I will always be here to love you. Forever. You are my sister.

My Beloved Mother
Tara D. Rivera

I love you Mom. You have a heart of gold. You've been through so much, there's a story to be told. A story so genuine, so original, so true that only a warrior such as yourself can subdue. A gem, a star, I can see it in your eyes. You have conquered so much, it's no surprise you can't disguise the laughter, the pain that you've endured. You will arise for your one who is wise, one who tries to keep the family ties, when all seems to go dim. You keep hope arrive. I love you mom, you are my angel, my love, send from the blue skies from heaven above. You are my queen that sits on her throne, made of pearls, diamonds and stone, as pure as white bone.

I love you Mom. You were always a good mother. You have always been there for me, sis and my brother. That's why there will never be another quite like you, ever never ever. I love you forever Mom, my beloved mother.

AT THE CAFÉ
SANDRA WILLIAMS

Sitting in the café with the music playing low, I get inspired to pick up my pen, and write a couple of lines. I'm feeling free to express softly. The lighting shining. A dimly lit shade. I feel like a fresh cup of coffee, two sugars and milk, with a chocolate chip cookie. My thoughts are ripe for this moment. A peaceful writing session in this café.

ELECTION DAY
GLORIA PAIGE

To the Voters:

Get up at 4 am. Arrive at 5 am at PS 54. A few workers already there. Police car pulls up to drop off police poll site envelope. Head inside to PS 54 into gym. Everyone greets each other. Get our instructions. Start setting up the polls. Confusion. Mostly everyone's first time. The coordinator has not yet arrived. It's 5:35 am. Voters arrive at 6 am. We're not ready. Finally everything's together. We're ready for work. 6 am voters come in. I'm at the lowest election district inspection table, where I'm the Chairperson. The other inspector I work with is Tanya who we also took the class with me is relieved. As we wait for voters, we chit chat. She is Greek and lives not far from me. We were talking about different types of food. She tells me she's on a Mediterranean diet where she limits consumption of meat. She also eats octopus and squid. It's after 2 pm. Tanya and I only got 2 voters so far. It's a really slow day. It's very quiet. 3 pm change of shift, for the police shift change for closing out the polls. The lucky guy who takes the scanner ballot box, the site return bag, large yellow scanner and the election night PMD return forms to the precinct. Police Officer Suthrie, very handsome, sexy, strong and a gun. I'm safe already. Oh, I forgot to tell you Tanya told me that work "gyro" in Greek is pronounced "yweero" and means "round." I met a lot of different people today, of all ethnicities – Jews, Spanish, African-American, White. All who came out to be counted.

WHAT FILLS MY WRITING
SHANNELY M. TRINIDAD

Young, I sought my way into writing.
I don't know how it happened or what made me want to write.
Growing up, I went through a lot.
Child abuse, child molestation
And being into my journal was my way of escape,
Escape into my own world.
Things seem brighter, better,
More me.
No hurt. No pain.
So writing filled me
The way I expressed myself on paper,
No one can take that way.
So I let it flow.
Let it go.
To think something so little as writing can fill me.

Sweet Space
Jeanne Byrne

The idea of having a place to write first came to me by "A Room of One's Own" by Virginia Woolf. It would be a room to think and write. It would be almost a "man cave" for woman. My ideal place would have a fireplace and smell like pine. It would have many plants and herbs. A perfect peace would be imbued with colors, scents and sounds of nature. I find this to be inspiring and comfortable. I could write about the past, present and future, all alone, in a sweet space.

A Person In a Place With a Problem
Holly M. Williams

My very first day in Claramont High Grade School.
All alone on this crisp sunny day,
8:30 in the morning
With only a small memory of remembering
How to get back home
With only a white tee shirt and tan blue denim jeans
And black and white Puma high top sneakers on.
That I felt very comfortable for the day.
It's so crowded on the platform at the Far Rockaway station.
Forgetting my backpack as I rushed off the train.
Oh my gosh, what am I going to do.
I can only think of all my personal belongings.
For instance, like my wallet, my phone
All vanished like a drop of a dime.
I'm so uptight right now, I could cry.
My memories just went blank for a few seconds.
And I'm still standing here wondering,
What can I do, or what should I do as I hold my head down,
asking God to make it reappear.
Hoping and praying that God guides me
    in the right direction and answers my prayers.
I'm only eleven and a half.
How could I be such a fool.
As I drifted slowly up the stairs,
Forgetting all about school,
Tears ran down my tired eyes,
Thinking how could life be so cruel.

Now I'm on my way home
But Mom doesn't get in 'till five.
As I paced up and down in front of my house for hours.
Finally Mom's just getting here.
So I explain to her, just how my day went.
She slowly hugged me tight
And said, go eat and get some sleep.
We will figure it out tomorrow,
'Cause tomorrow's another day.
As I return home from school the next afternoon,
Mom called me and said,
She has some good news.
The transit has your bag in the lost and found.
So come and pick up my bag real soon.
I hugged my mom with laughter and joy,
Saying to myself, Thank God
Life isn't really that cruel.

BELIEVE
JOYEIL GLOVER

Believe me when I say I won't hit you anymore. Believe me when I tell you, my little girls, that I am coming back for you. Trust and believe me, when I get paid, that I will soon get help for my addiction. Oh, please trust and believe me when I say that I will stop turning tricks. Now time has gone by, after all these things she said to plenty of people over the years. But you ask her, know you would stay proud and tall and say I told you one to, "believe me when I say that I was going to get things together. All I need to do was just to Believe in Myself." That's why I say "believe." You can accomplish so much if you just believe.

A NORMAL DAY
GLORIA PAIGE

A normal day is a day without chaos and confusion
A normal day is a day of peace without intrusion
A normal day is a day when you wake up
    and can smell the fresh air
When at times before you never really cared
A normal day is when you look up at the bright sun
And go outside and have some fun
A normal day is at the end of the night
When you snuggle under the covers oh so tight.

Lines
Celines Parra

Writing on these lines how beautiful and wonder if can be, to express your feelings and thoughts of happiness and sadness. These lines, arrowing each space can bring and give to feel them, and understand them and to express just about anything that can breath like the air we need, to eyes to see and our heart, to feel the beat. What a magical moment it brings to share these times with me.

TRIBE
SHANNELY M. TRINIDAD

Thinking over and over about this word TRIBE. It means so much, yet has one purpose. A group of people fighting for the same cause, helping another out for the same reasons. I consider myself part of one part of the tribe, standing for something, meaning something, feeling something, communicating something. Yet I'm the leader of it all. My perseverance, strength, thoughts, feelings, it's what I always talk about, it's what I always say. So let's fight. Let's stand the storm. Let's believe in the cause because the cause is greater. My Tribe, my success, my story, we are all here for one purpose, we withstand the reasons, we believe we can do this. We are the tribe. We are the leaders.

Dawn
Joyeil Glover

It was early morning when Mary stepped out of her door. With the mist on her skin and the cold wind against her body. As she began looking on the sun rising, she began to say, "it's going to be a fucked up day." All she could think about was Dawn! So Mary went back inside. She made her coffee and turned the shower on, and started her day. With that, she just kept saying to herself, "it's gonna be a fucked up day." As she started her car, the morning had come and the day was bright. Mary looked in the mirror and said to herself, it was only "Dawn."

WHERE WOULD I FIND A SPACE TO WRITE
BY TARA D. RIVERA

On a warm spring day in Central Park, hearing birds chirp, and the sound of squirrels, Scampering up the tree bark. Watching the light shimmer off the lake, like seeing diamonds in the ripples that the ducks make. Like a cool fall evening walking on the beach, As the sun begins to set way beyond reach then I see myself, starting at the pages of my book. There seems to be so much I have written from the trip I took. A trip of imagery, a world called imagination, that's where I find my best writing creation.

Where I can find peaceful dreams other than when I sleep at night but pleasant imagery is where I find my space to write.

Something for Richie
Tara D. Rivera

Like a child at heart while in your presence surrounded by your clutter of dolls and vintage clothing and infamous paintings of Hedy Lamarr, entering your perfect world, I felt like a star, a star that was never able to become, a life that I never had until you came along and showed me a better one. A life of love and true friendship, a battleship, a spaceship. We set the stage together, as we became one, a long life we promised that wouldn't ever be undone. Unity, destiny, eternity, I say to myself as I watch you slowly wither away. But you promised we'd be friends forever, you'd never go astray. Oh no, I think I'm going to cry. Where are you going, Richie? You're not ready to enter the sky but I'm not willing to let you go to that place. You appear to be slipping with such haste, where's the race? I need to see your sweet face. And then you go, I need to know, why? No no, not now. Am I being selfish maybe? It's your time to go. I glance upon your face and I can tell you're at peace. I finally see you're where you need to be. So I say, fly Richie fly, to that place way up high. You will always shine down on me. You are now my beautiful diamond in the sky. RIP Richard Rheem.

CULTURAL TRUTH
STEPHANIE KING

Writing about the biggest mistake ever made by us would consist of how the little word we know as "culture" has been defined. Seven letters have never caused as much confusion in one language. To even deny for a second that I wish to compete for the chance at the task at this point is to deny that I'm communicating in English. Our linguistic structures and syntax dominate the idea of material, both physical and written in an ideological struggle with ourselves. We don't have the "culture" to teach us what culture may possibly be without us, that information which is the truth but may not yet have taken embodiment. We acknowledge in our processes and systems that not all problems are solved, some may be unprovable, for sure we will never know everything. Until this "culture" wants for its inherent lack of a mind of its own we will have to retrieve this information to pass along by any means necessary a mind of truth will not exist, not to us, not from us to anyone else. It should be bigger and still empty, a void but not of ideation, opinions and distractedness. Those are misaligned thoughts that we simply allow into our culture.

TRIBE
JOYEIL GLOVER

Did you ever hear about this tribe called the Walkers? Well, their leader was named Jason. He looked after 2,000 people. They lived in the Amazon jungle. While there, he kept them protected and well-fed. Then there was this one moment when one of the children was playing and something happened. They had been living in the Amazon for a long time. Jason always would tell the young kids a story about a big mean bear that lived near by and liked to eat young boys and girls who didn't behave. He did this so the children would listen to their parents. While he was in the midst of telling his story to the children, a young little boy snuck off and had gotten lost. No one in the tribe noticed that he was missing until it was suppertime. His mother, who name is Joan, couldn't find her son, so she went to Jason and said, "I can't find my son." So Jason sent some of the tribe's men to go and look after the boy. They found him right under his favorite tree, where he always played. After that day on, Jason made sure that from that day forth, all the children would be looked after with a close eye. He prided himself with always making for his tribe was in great safety and never in danger.

A Person in a Place with a Problem
Tara D. Rivera

In the heart of the jungle where the ferocious live, she wanders aimlessly through the dirt barefoot and frightened that she may never find her way out. As she listens to the mighty roars of the winds scream into the hot, sticky, rainy, summer dawn, she looks around for an exit only to see the tree animals swinging through the vines. As the very skinny rain sprinkles about like a mist with the deep vegetation, she becomes drenched, her clothes sticking to her like a wet plastic bag with the air completely sucked out. She continues to walk, she is comfortable for a moment. As she begins to ponder in her comfortability, she finds that she is able to adjust. She is no longer afraid. She has forgotten the world outside of the jungle, where she once found peace and stability.

The misty rain subsides and the sun has gone down. She continues walking without ever noticing the beautiful sunset. It is now dark and all that is heard are the crickets singing, and the owl whooing. She is not afraid and continues walking as if she has now become one with this new universe only to find herself in the lion's den...

As she realizes that she has locked eyes on the almighty king of the jungle, she makes a run for safety. She runs so fast, she falls straight into a deep hole in the soil that has been covered with leaves. As she lay at the bottom, she anticipates how she would climb out. She looks up to see the pack on hungry lions leaping above her, then pure sounds of silence takes over as she thinks

Continued

to herself, how did it come to this. She makes a number of effortless attempts to climb out but fails every time. Finally, not aware of how long she has been confined, she makes her way out to greet day light, sun beaming, birds chirping and singing is music to her ears, and soon she forgets that she is lost and continues to explore the deep wooded dangerous jungle.

The rain is gone but the sun is at its highest. It is damp and humid, she has ventured for days forgetting to nourish, nurture her body. She is thirsty and dehydrated. She looks around and sees a stream of water, not realizing it was a mirage, she approaches the lovely stream of water, only finding herself in another scary yet familiar situation. She starts to run away from the water, tripping over the rocks and the old tree stump, she makes a clean getaway from the stampede of elephants that were being hunted by the hyenas, this time finding herself trapped in a cave that is blocked off by a huge boulder, caused by an avalanche, due to the stampede. This time it takes twice as long to get out and once she is out, she realizes she has spent half a lifetime running and seeking adventure, forgetting she was lost from the beginning, only to find herself in life threatening situations.

What, she wonders, does she do next?

GROW

A Beautiful Moment
Kaela Augustine

I am free! Today my shackles and cuffs were removed, never to return again. The raw groves of skin on my wrists and ankles can see, speak and breathe relief. All of my life is forgiven in this moment of redemption. Hall hath no fury like a jail cell. I've danced in the flames of a modern day Hell on Earth, to now taste a drop of Heaven. If angels truly do sing, right now I hear their tune booming through the lymph nodes of chickadees. This very moment, freedom sounds like laughter, cars speeding through traffic and cell phones ringing in the distance. Years of stress and fear sprout wings and take flight from the arc of my shoulder blades. The cool breeze welcomes me, and we dance together. We talk at our own pace, and in our own pattern. A single teardrop escaped from my old eyes, ran to the crevice of my mouth, and landed in the pool of my soul. I savor the flavors of joy and success. There's no place like home.

FAITH
Holly M. Williams

It's when all hope is
When you're at your weakest
But you have to be strong,
Just standing there all alone
From dusk to dawn.
Where is the spirit of faith,
It seems to take so long
When all hope is gone.
My ears are listening
And my mouth has no words.
It's such an uneasy feeling
That everything's gone wrong.
What did I do to deserve this,
All these mixed feelings inside.
I feel like a time bomb ticking
With no one to guide me or no place to hide.
I need someone to hold me and squeeze me,
And put my mind at ease
And at the last moment,
Faith just comes strolling along.
And now there is peace.
Within.

My Chance is Now
Shannely M. Trinidad

My chance is now to learn.
My chance is now to change.
My chance is now. My chance is now.
To change. To learn right from wrong.
To live in the now. To have a chance to change.
To make a choice that will better me, my future.
To have a chance to change. Prove myself now.

MY WORK
ELAINE G. SIMMONS

My work is...keeping my faith in God;
And that I'm in the right place in my life.

My work is...to love myself enough to stay clean and sober –
And to try to have something in my life.

My work is ...to "listen" so that I can really receive –
That might just save my life.

My Work
Louise Boriello

My work is to work on myself.
My work is to stay sober.
My work is to help people.
My work is to get help for myself.
My work is never done.

THIS IS A STORY ABOUT PERSEVERANCE

JOYEIL GLOVER

When you have been hurt, abused and can't trust anyone, you start to doubt yourself. But when I picked myself up, cried, talked about my problems, I began to get "perseverance." You want to know how it felt? It felt good, like the world was lifted off my shoulders. Like God has made it to a new born child of his all over again. I never thought that things could feel this good. Perseverance is a wonderful thing to have. Once you get that taste of it, you would never want to give it up. Remember what it is ladies and gentlemen, it is perseverance.

My Best Friend Gloria
Gloria Paige

Gloria,

I am writing you because I am tired of you putting yourself down. Of thinking yourself unworthy, believing no one could ever love you. Your self-esteem is so low that you are afraid to believe you are beautiful inside and out. Forget about the scars. Don't you know you have a beautiful heart? I see how you are with people. I see how you do for others before yourself and that you are sincere from your heart, not asking for anything in return. You are the sweetest person I know. I want you to know that I love you, God loves you and others will love you too. Your love, kind heart and humble spirit are what I find most amazing. What I want you to do Gloria when you get up, before you take a shower, is to take off all your clothes in front of the mirror and look at yourself, scars and all and tell yourself that I love you. Every Day. All the Time. Keep saying this until you believe it because you are beautiful. Do things for yourself. Get your hair and nails done. Buy yourself a gift and let yourself be open to receive unconditional love in all areas until you are ready to love yourself. Until you do, you honestly can't love anyone else. So in closing, I love you very much, just the way you are, and I will keep loving until you love yourself.

Love Your Best Friend Forever,
Gloria

FREEDOM
LOUISE BORRIELLO

My days at Serendipity are over.
I'm finally going home.
I feel free,
Independent,
Ready to go on with my life.
The demons are gone —
Replaced with positive energy.
I feel free and oh,
What a feeling it is.

ME
Tara D. Rivera

I am broken and need to be fixed, believing my own lies, master manipulator, self defiant, searching for answers within oneself. Do I love myself? Do I distrust myself? Once I believe I could change the world, solve everyone else's problems, heal everyone else's pain. Am I capable of changing the world? If not, then who is? Am a martyr, a rebel without a cause? I used to think so. Do I live in the past by allowing every tragedy or bad situation to be like a facsimile in my memory bank? So many shattered memories. Abandonment, loss, are they really shattered? Then why do I continue to relive them? Do I really live in the past or is it an excuse to move on and stay in stagnation? Letting my mind go completely blank....oh! I get it now. I'm not broken, nor am I a liar, or a manipulator. I was merely a hurt person trying to get out of a bad situation, I do love myself as much as I love others and that does not make my a martyr. I can trust myself. I do know today that I may not be able to change the world but I can make a difference. I don't have to die a super hero and that facsimile has been shredded, erased. I am not broken nor do I need to be fixed. I'm exactly who I need to be. I'm just me.

A Woman's Courage
Celine Parra

A woman of courage and strength,
A woman of inner wisdom,
A survivor at heart.
The woman who still struggles through
Challenges and obstacles that come her way
To strive for that self-freedom.
A conservative woman
Of many experiences and existence in life,
A woman of hope, faith and love.

EXCITEMENT
GLORIA PAIGE

How exciting it is to be free from addiction,
To see and smell the beautiful flowers
Where as in addiction there was no scent at all.
How exciting it is to see birds with the rainbow
    colors on their necks,
Where as in addiction they dirty and dingy.
How exciting it is to wake to the
bright, yellow sun,
In the crystal clear blue sky
Peaking through the white cotton-like clouds,
Where as in addiction everyday and everything is filled
    with darkness and drear.
Ah, and how exciting it is just to wake up and
    have a chance to live again.

DAWN
TINA ARMSTRONG

The dawn of your beauty comes from deep within,
The dawn of your beauty is why I can call you my friend.

We had our differences, which made us strong.
Only two women can change a difference into a song.

The dawn of your laughter, makes me smile.
The dawn of your tears I hold inside.

God brought our roads together,
which no man can take apart.
The dawn of your friendship, I will forever hold in my heart.
I thank God for our friendship, it seems to have just begun.
The dawn of your beauty is like the rising of the sun.
So let's continue to sing praises to God through songs,
Because you will forever me my friend Dawn...

DETERMINATION
Dominique Allen

Determined to fly
Determined to believe
In all things I shall achieve.
Determined to soar
Determined to fly
Like an eagle above the skies.
We should all take flight and be determined
Determined to win this fight.
Determined to the be real me,
A real mother,
We all should believe we can achieve.
So reach for the sky
And fly,
Fly Lady Eagles Fly.
Even with a broken wing
You can fly.
Just look at all your lady eagles
(who thought they couldn't)
Rosa Parks, Harriet Tubman and Madame CJ Walker.

MURAL
THE SERENDIPITY WRITERS

The Madonna is a perplexed portrait
Throughout the world all artists sought it
She has no expression just design
No sign of sadness hidden inside
No smile although all viewers know
There's something there that doesn't show
Expenseless is her lasting gleam
No one has yet found what she dreamed.

That was good luck.
Surviving the storm
New beginnings make you nervous,
But each one has a purpose.
 (Oh, how I hate that word).
You were beautiful and happy?
A smile. Now that is torn in pieces,

Do you remember how we laughed and sang.

I'm having a hard time adjusting to change
Life threw me a hard ball
Their sharp fingernails torn in my skin.
So I can move on.
Peaceful could I have seen.
We as newborns know nothing Of the world.
Have serenity
Within

Continued

Toward
What
We were raised to be.
I felt that calm

I knew that from what I learned
Growing up
Everyday
Is a new day.

Ready to go on with my life.
The demons are gone –
Replaced with positive energy.
What a feeling it is.

Buttery – Lightweight – Burnt – Soft Feeling

Waiting
To find itself in the world.
Looking
Be needed.
Of the lies that are said that, There's something better on the other side.

We the world
Stay wailing.
Children wailing.
Adults wailing.
All the wailing and no change.
Wailers wail on and nobody to hear why.
Why the high.

Apart
I cried into
The rage in wind.
I beg for death to come for me.

In sadness I fall into the burning flames, and
Rise
In silent prayer I gain strength,
for Jesus was beside me in my soul.
I had no fear,
My heartbeat to a calm melody, and
There

Wailing on
Takes me to destiny
And reminds me off hell
So that I can guide my soul.

Icicles
Melting me away.
My work is loving people.
My work is being a mom.
My work is work.
This is a letter to let you know, you are not alone.
Recovery, it's how you make your life story.
Who you put in as your characters and play it out.
Recovery can take you anywhere.
So cold to my feelings.
Cold!
When would it go away.
So I can feel warm once again.
My work is to stay away from
People, places and things.
My work is the pass the message over.

And I did.
And that I'm in the right place in my life.

My work is…to love myself enough
And to try to have something in my life.

Continued

My work is...to "listen" so that I can really
receive –
That might just save my life.
My work is to help people.
Mr. Big Stuff,
Who do you think you are.
Everybody's fundamental belongings
If you were born acrobatic
You'd have a missing line.

Acknowledgements

As a small, grassroots organization, NY Writers Coalition relies on the generous support of those dedicated to getting the voices of those who have been silenced heard. Many thanks go to our foundation, government, and corporate supporters, without whom this writing community and publication would not exist: Allianz GI, Amazon.com, the Kalliopeia Foundation, the National Endowment for the Arts, the New York City Department of Cultural Affairs, and the offices of New York City Council Members Laurie Cumbo and Corey Johnson. NYWC programming is also made possible by the New York State Council on the Arts with the support of Governor Andrew Cuomo and the New York State Legislature.

We rely heavily on the support of individual NYWC members and attendees of our annual Write-A-Thon. In addition, members of our Board of Directors have kept this vital, rewarding work going year after year: Louise Crawford, Marian Fontana, Sandy Huang, Matthew Krejcarek, Lisa Smith, Jonathan Tasini, and NYWC Founder and Executive Director Aaron Zimmerman.

The Serendipity Writers would also like to thank the Serendipity community, especially to the staff members' whose honesty and support pushes them forward every day: To Ms. Alexander, who has opened the arms of this program to their recovery; to Ms. Armstrong for guiding them through the right path; to Ms. Hammonds for being a reliable and understanding counselor; to Ms. Santiago, for the enlightening assignments and trips; to Ms. Cruz for creating a structure that allows them to grow; to Ms. Johnson, for keeping an alert, compassionate eye over them at night; to Ms. Greaves for opening their creativity with arts and crafts; to Ms. Cook for introducing them to the world of financial management; to Ms. Camacho for keeping their stomachs happy and full; to Ms. Blakery for making sure they have all they need to keep a tidy and clean house; to Ms. Foster for the sage advice; to Ms. Charlton for bringing lessons that open their minds. Thank you all. Your generosity and wisdom will not be forgotten. We would also like to thank Colleen Breslin, NYWC's volunteer workshop leader, who was instrumental in making this book happen, plus the dedicated workshop members and contributors at the Serendipity Program.

BY JEANNE BYRNE

About
NY Writers Coalition

NY Writers Coalition (NYWC) is a 501(c)(3) non-profit organization that creates opportunities for formerly voiceless members of society to be heard through the art of writing.

One of the largest community-based writing organizations in the country, we provide free, unique, and powerful creative writing workshops throughout New York City for people from groups that have been historically deprived of voice in our society, including at-risk, disconnected, and LGBT youth, homeless and formerly homeless people, those who are incarcerated and formerly incarcerated individuals, war veterans, people living with disabilities, cancer, and other major illnesses, immigrants, seniors, and many others.

For more information about NYWC programs and NY Writers Coalition Press publications visit
WWW.NYWRITERSCOALITION.ORG

www.ingramcontent.com/pod-product-compliance
Lightning Source LLC
Chambersburg PA
CBHW040907160426
43195CB00033B/108